# Prayer in Poetry For The Christian Teenager

**ALSO BY VICKY ANDRIOTIS:**

**PRAYER IN POETRY**

**PRAYER IN POETRY
FOR THE CHRISTIAN MOTHER**

**PRAYER IN POETRY – MORE EXPRESSIONS
OF FAITH**

**PRAYER IN POETRY – THE ANTHOLOGY**

Vicky Andriotis
# Prayer in Poetry
## for the
## Christian Teenager

Published by
Vicky Spyrou-Andriotis
Connecticut, USA

Copyright © 2009 by Vicky Spyrou-Andriotis
All Rights Reserved

No part of this book may be reproduced in any
manner whatsoever without written permission,
except in the case of brief quotations embodied in
critical articles or reviews.

Published 2009 by Vicky Spyrou-Andriotis

Printed and bound in the
United States of America
ISBN-10: 0-9821808-3-7
ISBN-13: 978-0-9821808-3-9

Prayer In Poetry For The Christian Teenager
www.vickyandriotis.com

Cover and Book Design – Vicky Spyrou-Andriotis

Images or photography that may be used in this book:
Copyright 2009 Vicky Spyrou-Andriotis

Scripture taken from the New King James Version®.
Copyright © 1982 by Thomas Nelson, Inc. Used by
permission. All rights reserved.

Dedicated to Him, for it is His words to us that give us courage, hope, and wisdom.

Written for the youth of today so that, with faith, they might become the hope of tomorrow.

# Contents

| | |
|---|---|
| Temptation | 15 |
| This Heart | 16 |
| When I Am | 17 |
| Lead Me | 18 |
| When I Call | 19 |
| This Day | 20 |
| Today | 21 |
| Gossip | 22 |
| Goodbye Friend | 23 |
| Your Love for Me | 24 |
| To Be Understood | 25 |
| Friends | 26 |
| Not Alone | 27 |
| Achieve | 28 |
| Needs of the World | 29 |
| I Believe | 30 |
| Differences | 31 |
| The Beginning | 32 |
| To See | 33 |
| While I Change | 34 |
| No Fear | 35 |
| My Journey | 36 |
| What Is Today? | 37 |
| Dearest Mother | 38 |
| You Are Love | 39 |
| That Is My Faith | 40 |
| When Tomorrow Comes | 41 |
| Your Words, My Prayers | 42 |
| Be Near Me | 43 |
| My Youth Is My Strength | 44 |
| A World Without Love | 45 |

| | |
|---|---|
| THIS IS ME | 46 |
| STEPPING STONES | 47 |
| YOUR NAME | 48 |
| MOUNTAINS | 49 |
| YOUTH | 50 |
| EVERY | 51 |
| BITTERSWEET | 52 |
| INTO THE FIRE | 53 |
| HOPE OF TOMORROW | 54 |
| BEING ME | 55 |
| YOU EMBRACE ME | 56 |
| THE CURE FOR WORRY | 57 |
| WHISPERS | 58 |
| HEAL ME | 59 |
| YOUR GIFT TO US | 60 |
| BRAVE | 61 |
| ERRORS & FORGIVENESS | 62 |
| COME CLOSER THEN | 63 |
| HOPE TO BE | 64 |
| KNOWLEDGE AND UNDERSTANDING | 65 |
| YOU ARE | 66 |
| A HEART THAT ACHES | 67 |
| INTO THE WORLD | 68 |
| LOOKING FOR HEROES | 69 |
| SINS OF OUR PAST | 70 |
| REMIND ME | 71 |
| THERE ARE DAYS | 72 |
| IN TIMES | 73 |
| DREAMS AND HOPE | 74 |
| MY SHIELD | 75 |
| YOUR NAME I CALL | 76 |
| GOOD MORNING | 77 |
| GIFTS ABOUND | 78 |

| | |
|---|---|
| Your Choices | 79 |
| This Struggle | 80 |
| There I Am | 81 |
| Alright | 82 |
| Limitless | 83 |
| In This Day, I Pray | 84 |
| To Speak to You | 85 |

"Let no one despise your youth, but be an example to the believers in word, in conduct, in love, in spirit, in faith, in purity." 1 Timothy 4:12 NKJV™

## TEMPTATION

O Lord
Let my heart remain a stranger to temptation
Let it laugh in the face of the youthful
transgressions and desires
That lead me away from You

That they seem foolish
And ordinary
To a life
Meant for the extraordinary
As long as I remain
Pure of heart
And work the deeds
That lead me back to
You

## THIS HEART

Help me to place
Kindness in my heart
Where anger has been
Let bitterness fade
And love remain

Teach me to forgive
And allow forgiveness
To erase
The hurt caused by those I love

Guide them to understand my sorrow
That they might take care
Not to hurt
This heart
Again
That they treat it with care
And gentleness
And that kindness
Be their guide
And mine

Amen

## When I Am

God
When I am afraid
Please give me courage

When I feel sadness
Please bring me joy

When I am tired
Allow me to rest

And when I am lonely
Bring me the comfort of those
I love

And Lord
When I feel like things
Aren't moving in the right direction
I pray for tomorrow
And
A
Better day

## LEAD ME

Heavenly Father
Who watches over me
Cares for me
Loves me

I pray
That you lead me
When I feel I might be lost

I pray
That I feel Your guiding hand
When I'm not sure where to go

I believe
That You will light my path
And that wherever You lead me
There
I Will follow

Amen

## WHEN I CALL

Lord
When I call
Please
answer

When I fall
Please
Catch me

If I'm lost
Please
Find me

When I'm cold
Please
Warm me

I thank You
Lord
For watching over me
Protecting me
And caring for me

Amen

## This Day

My Lord, Jesus
To You I pray
For a peaceful day
One filled with happiness
One filled with You
Filled with Your love

I pray for a day
Without anger
Or conflict
One without sin

And I thank You
For this day
So that I can be
Once again
The best
Of me

Amen

## TODAY

Today
Is a day
Full of promise

Today
Is a day
I will make my very own

I will be joyful
And recognize
All it has to offer

And I will give praise to God
For the opportunities in this day

I will take the time
To see each one
And gratefully accept
Those given to me

For today
Is a day
Full of promise

## GOSSIP

Lord
Why should the words that others say
Affect me so?
It is simply
Chatter

I know the gifts that I possess
They are God given
And I thank You

I pray you help to stifle this noise
That only serves to separate us

Help to remove the malice from the hearts of
my enemies
And let love prevail
That we learn to treat each other
With kindness
And sensitivity
That we find a common ground
Where we can live peacefully
Joyfully
Together

## GOODBYE FRIEND

As the time draws near
When we must part ways
Remember always
That God crossed our paths
For a reason
And though oceans may come between us
Or miles and miles of land
They can not separate
Lives
That God saw fit to bring together

I pray your journey brings you closer to a
life
Full of love
And laughter
And I thank God
For the gift of the time
We had
Together

## Your Love for Me

It is Your love I feel
Your hand upon my shoulder
And I remind myself
Of the sacrifices
You've made
Because of Your love
For me

And I realize
That to honor You
And Your sacrifices
I must love myself
I must understand my worth
I must realize my gifts
My abilities
And use them
In ways
That show my gratitude
And love
For You
And for
Myself

## TO BE UNDERSTOOD

Lord
I pray to be seen for who I am
And loved for who I can be
I hope
I pray
For I am gentle
And kind
And possess a heart
That is ready to love
A mind that is at peace
And full of thoughts that would please You

And so
I pray that my actions
And my words
Stem from a heart
That is pure
And seeks
Only
To be understood

## FRIENDS

These brothers and sisters
These spirits, like mine that
You have placed beside me
To walk with me
To lift me when I fall
To hold my hand
When I am afraid
To lend an ear
To lend a hand
To say a word
That makes a difference
In the moment
In the day
Or in my life

These kindred spirits
These friends who follow me through life
Laughing
Protecting
Guiding
For these friends
I pray

And for these friends
I thank You

## NOT ALONE

I am not alone
You surround me
You are the comforting word
The sun on my face
The music that I hear

I am not alone
I speak
And You hear
I pray
And You listen

I tell You my dreams
I tell You my fears
You are the rainbow in the sky
The love in my heart
The cure for loneliness
The peace
That I find
And I know
That I
Am not
Alone

## ACHIEVE

To achieve
What I am capable of
To recognize the gifts
That I possess
To find my true calling
Early in life
So that I may serve
You
I pray

To succeed in things
That have an impact
Make a difference
And change the world
For the better
I pray

I pray that my achievements
Please You
For then I will know
That I
Have truly
Succeeded

## NEEDS OF THE WORLD

Lord
Help me to look toward my future
And anticipate
The needs of my world

Grant me the abilities required to serve
mankind
For in serving Your people
I serve You

Help me to understand what is necessary to
help those
Around me
Friends and strangers alike
Those who inhabit my world
Those who hope in You
And let me be
The help they need

## I Believe

I believe
That I am just as I was meant to be
I believe
That I am as good on the outside
As I am on the inside
In these things
I am sure
Because it is God
Who has created me
And He creates all things
Perfect in their own way

I am clever
I am kind
I am selfless
And caring
I am strong
And courageous
And I possess a heart as good as any

I believe
That I am blessed
And I believe
That I am who I am meant to be
In His eyes
And in mine

## DIFFERENCES

God above
Heavenly Father
Help us to see
Open our eyes to the things we share
To those things we have in common
As they outnumber
Those that make us different from each
other

We crave to be unique
Yet do not always accept those who are
Show us how to celebrate each other
Learn from each other
Be with one another
And appreciate
What each of us has to offer
And understand
That each of us
Is a child
Of
God

## THE BEGINNING

Laugh
Smile
Rejoice, my friend
Don't you know how blessed we are?
This is our time
The days of innocence
The time of freedom
Before the world's trials
Come to greet us

Our youth
Our chance to learn
To grow
To begin
To become

So laugh
Smile
Rejoice in our blessings
Pray for tomorrow
And be glad for these beginnings

## TO SEE

I will
Be still
For a moment
And truly allow my eyes
To see
Only then
Will I appreciate how truly remarkable
My
Life
Is
And will be

I am aglow
This simple realization
Appreciation
Awareness
Fills me with hope
And gratitude
And I am struck
And amazed
By visions, so extraordinary
And I thank the Lord
For placing me
In the midst of it
All

## WHILE I CHANGE

For the strength to face my future
For the courage to walk towards the
unknown
For a loving voice to guide me
For loving arms to hold me
While I change
And grow
Into who I am meant to become
To You
I pray

For the boldness to move forward
And the humility
To understand when to step back

For signs to follow
And You to lead the way
As I move through my life
I pray

## NO FEAR

Love
Out loud
Love
With all you are
And all you have
Love
Others as yourself
Even He commands it
Expects it
Requires it

There is no fear in love[⊕]
Nor should you fear to love
Give it freely
Without expectations
Or conditions
Give without knowing if it will be returned
There is no fear in love
Only your heart's
Reward

---

[⊕] The Holy Bible (NKJV™) 1 John 4:18

## My Journey

The roads I've yet to travel
The dreams I've yet to dream of
I pray You walk beside me
I pray You lead and guide me
I pray Your will be done
Through me
For me
Because of me

That my journey is pleasant
My load is light
My works are many
My mistakes are few
I ask

That the road ahead is paved
And unobstructed
So that my journey is peaceful
I pray

## WHAT IS TODAY?

It is for you to notice the stars
For you to hear the voice that calls you
Calls to you
And calls upon you
To fulfill, and achieve
To remind you that the future is coming
What is today?

A chance to turn another page
Another chance
To pray
Another chance to change
To believe
To turn sorrow into sunlight
To build bridges you have burned
To move forward
Without leaving your soul behind

What is today?
Another chance
To find
Your way

## Dearest Mother

Have I caused you trouble?
Am I the cause of your fears?
Please
Forgive me
For it is unintentional
A product
A result of this search that brings me
Nearer to who I am

Put your worry aside
And know
That when I seem to be lost
He leads me to my path again
And though I might err
And seem to stray further away
He will guide me safely back
For He was in the thoughts
That led me there

## YOU ARE LOVE

As I begin this search
I come to understand
That I needn't search very far

For
I see You in a mother's eyes
I see You in a child's smile
I feel You in a friend's embrace
In the hands that I hold
And those that hold mine

You are love
Warm
And pure
Clear as day
Brighter than the sun itself

You are love
Deep within all that I see
And so I needn't search very far
I've only but to look
And there
I'll
See

## THAT IS MY FAITH

This light
It shines like the flames of a million candles

This light
I see in the eyes of those who have faith

This light
Inside of me
It gives me strength
It is the food that fuels my soul
It drives me
And warms me

The strength of a million candles pales in
comparison
To the light
That is
My faith

## WHEN TOMORROW COMES

Don't live your life
Concerned with foolish things
Do not be ruled by emotions harmful to you
Consumed
By hate and jealousy
Rage and envy

When tomorrow comes
He will know what's in your heart

When tomorrow comes
He will seek those who have lived
Their lives
In
Love
In
Patience
And those who have lived joyfully
Meaningfully
And gratefully

And so be sure
That is you
When tomorrow comes

## Your Words, My Prayers

Words
Tossed about recklessly
Landing
Painfully
Upon innocent hearts

Words
Meant to harm and antagonize
Taunting
Piercing one's spirit
Damaging the self

But Your words
With courage and faith
Form the prayers
That shield my spirit
Guarding and protecting me
Mending my heart

Your words are the prayers
That heal
A broken
World

## BE NEAR ME

With You
My fear subsides
With You
I know comfort and hope
Solace
My troubles dissipate
Solutions are clearer

I pray
Be near me
Your faithful child
That my mind may always be clear enough
to understand the answers You provide

Be near me
So that I am reminded of how all things are
possible
Always
As long as You are near me

## My Youth Is My Strength

Lord
That my youth be my strength
And not my weakness
I pray

That my conduct and wisdom
Be of one who is twice my years
But that I remain as pure and innocent as
one who is young, still
One who is eager to learn
And follow
One who is not yet influenced
By a world yet unseen
Whose natural instincts
To love
Forgive
And nurture
Have not been corrupted
Or erased
By a world that is jaded
And weary

Lord, for this I pray

## A WORLD WITHOUT LOVE

There is a truth to be told
And to be understood
A truth for a kinder
Selfless
World
That love
Should not be a struggle
Nor should it be a chore
Nor
Should you keep it from others

It should be found
And followed
Received openly
And given often
And freely
It should be in our actions
And in our reactions

For a world without love
Is a world
Without
Him
In it

## THIS IS ME

I find life
Within myself
Within my world
Because I have found You

I have found the reasons
For all that I have questioned
And misunderstood
Because I've found You

I can spread my wings
I have found my courage
I can say that I'm free
Because I have found You

I can say "This is me"
I've found my way
And a place to be
A place for us who've longed to know
A place to be grateful
And a place to say
"This is me"

## STEPPING STONES

These are our moments
Fragile
Fleeting
The stepping stones of life
Placed before us to be remembered
Yet left behind for the lives that await us
Lives of purpose
Driven by God
Driven by our faith in Him

We will be mindful
And grateful for these moments
For they serve to shape who we are

But we will be driven
By the thought
Of who we shall become

## YOUR NAME

I think, and stop
In this moment
It is the sound of your name
That inspires me most

I think
And am comforted
By the thought of You
Your name brings joy to the lips that speak
It
The mind that knows It
And the heart that believes in It

I stop
And I think
How just the sound of Your name
Makes life
So much
Sweeter

## MOUNTAINS

Another mountain to climb
Sometimes they seem insurmountable
And I can not imagine the other side
And I can not imagine
That there is a path that can lead me there
And I realize
That my mind is closed
To the possibilities
That come with faith
And love
In You

For the mountain will be moved
That my future may be opened wide
For You have laid it at my feet
And with faith
I shall move closer to it

## YOUTH[⊕]

Oh youth
You are but a tool
We use
Often unwisely
Foolishly we seek
Things of little significance
And carelessly endanger
Our souls and bodies

Youth
You blind us to the truth
And often keep us from
The path
That leads us to our true
Reward

You are a gift
To be used
Wisely and with great care
So that when you are gone
Wisdom remains

---

[⊕] From "Prayer in Poetry –More Expressions of Faith".
Used By Permission. Copyright ©2009 V. Andriotis

## EVERY

Every Hope
Comes from above
Every thought
Is suddenly clear
Every day
Is more of a blessing
That the day before

Every time
I stop and listen
Take a moment
And truly listen
I find I understand
What I hadn't understood before
Things that matter more than I knew
And I become
A minute wiser
A little kinder
And
Warmer
Still
Every time

## BITTERSWEET

Oh, these days
Bittersweet
Some things are lost, left behind
And yet, there is still so much we have to gain

But it feels as though it all moves along without you

And changes persist
And fear settles in

But it can not overwhelm you
It can not overcome you
It will be crushed by the weight of your faith
It can not keep you from your future
For He is by your side
And you are by His own design
Perfect in your own way

And though these days may be bittersweet
Look toward what can be gained
And do not dwell
On what's been left behind

## INTO THE FIRE

It's like I'm walking on hot sand
Open road before me
It burns beneath my feet, and I wonder
How long I can bear it
How long before I surrender

And then, I am reminded that the sun still
shines upon my face
And still lights my way
And I know I must be grateful
And I know I must be hopeful
And I realize that I can move forward

And so
Into the fire I walk
Into the fire today
But I trust that I'll walk through it
Like I did
Just yesterday

## Hope Of Tomorrow

Are we
The hope of tomorrow?
Are we to be the answer to the prayers
That were prayed
Today?

With our eyes, open
And our ears, listening
And our hearts, willing
A chance exists
That the knowledge, and wisdom, and love
we obtain today
Might someday help another
Might someday build the world
As God intended it to be
Helping others find their way
And find the light inside
That God
Put
There

## BEING ME

A place
To be myself
A time
To feel how I feel
Without words
Without wondering
If I
Am enough

A place
With You
Where I know acceptance
Love
With You I can simply be
And know that I bring You joy
Just
By being
Me

## You Embrace Me

You embrace me
Even when I feel
I haven't done what I should

You still embrace me
As if to say
You understand
It's alright
I can try again

Mistakes I have made
But know that forgiveness awaits
Should I choose to ask for it

And so, You embrace me
Comfort me
And guide me
Knowing that all I need
Is to try again

## THE CURE FOR WORRY

I worry, Lord
But know that worry can not resolve
Can not fix
The things that worry me

Somewhere within me
I hear You say
"Have faith."
And I know that this is the answer
The cure for worry
The remedy for fear

Faith
Simple
Powerful
Faith
Is my antidote
And my salvation

Faith
So that my worry
Is
No more

## WHISPERS

There are whispers
Lord
They float to my ears
And make their way into my conscience
In the place where Your words reside
And it is there that they are pushed aside
It is there that I hear You
And know that those whispering
Would lead me away from You

And so
The whispers are hushed
As are those who speak them
And I realize
That a step away from them
Is one step
Closer
To
You

## HEAL ME

Heal me
O Lord
Heal me
From the pain in my heart
To the pain in my soul
From the pains that are physical
To those
Emotional

I pray
O Lord
To be healed

I believe
With all that I am
That my prayer will be heard
That my prayer will be answered
And that
Your mercy
Is my
Salvation

## Your Gift To Us

Time is Your gift to us
And in this
Our appetites are insatiable
There will never be enough
We can not be satisfied

But
We are innocent of gluttony
For it is with great purpose
And joy
That we partake for this gift
Your gift
To us

And so, Lord, I pray
Do not fault us
For our unquenchable thirst for time
For it is You
Who created
Something so sweet and irresistible
To us all

## BRAVE

Brave
I step into life
Eager
Willing

Brave
Into the untried
And the unknown
Brave and undeterred by my own fears
Knowing You are beside me
Knowing You are my strength
I remain brave
There is nothing to fear

So I pray
As I step forward into life
And know
That fears aside
Your will
Be done

## Errors & Forgiveness

Though I sin
Lord, do not resist me
I understand my errors
And seek forgiveness

Though I sin
My intentions are good
My heart is generous with love
It is full with faith
And seeks absolution

And though I may sin
I steer myself toward the truth
And the light
And away from the sins
I abhor

## COME CLOSER THEN

Are you lost?
Gather near Me

Have you forgotten where you always
belong?
Come closer then

Is it love that you seek?
I Am here

Come home again
And find your purpose
Come closer to Me and find your love, my
love for you

Find your purpose
My purpose for you
With Me, you are always home

Come closer then

## Hope To Be

Love and patience
Kindness
Which is my strength?
What mark will I make?

Generous
Honest
Humble
How shall I be known?

I pray, by all of these
For the Good Book tells me so
Compassionate and honorable
With my faith planted firmly in my heart

This is who I hope to be
And whom I've begun
To become

## KNOWLEDGE AND UNDERSTANDING

I wish to understand, Lord
To feel
And truly understand

May the Holy Spirit touch me
Move me
Inspire me
So that Your words to us
Come to mind with every breath I take
And word that I speak

I wish to understand , Lord
So that I can be freed by the knowledge
The understanding
That it is Your will
That will
Be done

## You Are

You are my light in the dark

You are the cure for my pain

You are my guide when I am lost

You are the hope in all that fails

You are the smile when there is sadness

You are the warmth in a world that is often cold

You are the sun on my face
And the shadow that walks beside me

You are the love in my heart
And the contentment
Comfort
And peace
In my soul

## A HEART THAT ACHES

Is it your heart that aches?
A heart that aches
Has known love
Love is what He
Commands
Expects
Requires of us
And so
Rejoice in knowing
That in this
You did abide

A heart that aches
Has known love
And will heal
When it
Finds love
Again

## INTO THE WORLD

As I venture out today
Into a world, unfamiliar to me
I pray for courage
And the ability to navigate my way
Through this sea
Of uncertainty

That I take what comes with ease
That I handle well the things
I can not control
That fear escapes me
And trouble eludes me
That I accept challenges
Willingly, joyfully
And that I am always aware of Him
And that He guides me

As I venture out into the world today
I pray
Be near me

## LOOKING FOR HEROES

A constant need to find heroes in our lives
My search
Leads me to You
No other compares
No other is required
For You are our guiding light
Our example
Of all things good
And all things possible
Of all that can be achieved
And all the rewards that can be had

You
Protecting
Guiding
Teaching
And saving

You
Are
My Hero

## Sins Of Our Past

Foolish
The choices of our youth
And yet, we are accountable
And with age
Will repent

I pray
That with hearts full of You
Our choices are wiser
Thoughtful
And without need for regret

I pray that our impulses
Are curbed by the thought of their
consequences
So that our futures are not spent
Correcting
The sins
Of our pasts

## REMIND ME

When my vision has clouded
And I am losing sight
Of the goals at hand
And my way is uncertain
And unclear
Remind me Lord
Of You

When I am sinking further away
From Your plan for me
And my foolishness
Has taken hold of our future

Remind me, Lord
Of You

## THERE ARE DAYS

There are days
When I forget
To thank You

There are days
When my thoughts
Wander away from You

Sometimes days have gone by
Before I realize
That I haven't spoken to You
Asked You
Praised You

For these days
I ask Your forgiveness
For my selfishness
I repent
And to You
I shall always be grateful

## IN TIMES

I have found
In times of sorrow
In times of fear
In times of worry
In times of uncertainty
I have found
In all these times
The hope
Of You

In the cold of night
In the darkness of my soul
I find that I am sheltered
By the hope
Of You

Comforted
Inspired
Soothed
In the hope
Of You
I have found
Solace

## DREAMS AND HOPE

What dreams are these I carry?
The dreams my life might hold

But
They are no more than prayers
Not yet prayed

They are no more than thoughts
Drifting away

That
Once prayed
Turn from dreams
Into the hope
Of the life
I
Can begin
to lead

## MY SHIELD

You are my shield
My protection from all who seek to harm me
From all who might dampen my spirit
And test my faith

You are my shield
From a world
Sometimes unkind
From places of loneliness
Darkness
And those who thrive on fear

You are my shield
And I am filled with Your spirit
It is my armor
Against fools and the faithless
In them
Fear shall be victorious
While in You
My heart survives

## YOUR NAME I CALL

In joy
In pain
In need
And in abundance
It is Your name that I call

In moments of confusion
In moments of clarity
Through tears
And through laughter
It is Your name that I call

When all seems out of place
When all is as it should be
When what seems random
Is Your will
Hear me, Lord
For it is Your name
That I call

## GOOD MORNING

Good morning, Lord!
As my feet touch the floor
As my eyes
Glimpse the sunlight
As my mind
Awakes from its slumber
It is You I greet
Whom I seek
You
Who occupies my thoughts
First and before all others
As my day begins

As I wipe the sleep from my eyes
You are the first on my lips
As I greet You
Thank You
Praise You
As I honor You
By being
This day
All that You
Expect me to be

## Gifts Abound

Being made by God Almighty
Created in His image
Created
So that His will is done
How can I question
Or doubt myself?

I am His very own creation
I am God made
And therefore
Exactly as I am supposed to be

And for this I am grateful
In me His gifts abound
And I shall use
Each one
To live a life
Worthy
Of having them

*Prayer in Poetry for the Christian Teenager*

## YOUR CHOICES[⊕]

In the eyes of she who raised you
In the heart of the one you call mother
Know that you are
The one
And the only

The one for whom her life revolves
The one whom she would give it for
Easily
Freely
Lovingly

And when you are choosing your actions
Or considering your deeds
Or searching for the right words to speak
Think first of God
Then her
And know that you have chosen
Admirably

---

[⊕] From "Prayer In Poetry For The Christian Mother".
Used By Permission. Copyright ©2008 V. Andriotis

## This Struggle[⊕]

Do not feel that your life's a struggle
Rejoice in what you have
And understand
That God knows your needs
As well as your burdens

You must believe
That God will provide
That He knows your fears
And your sorrows
Your aspirations
Your dreams

Believe that there are blessings
Meant for you
Believe
With all you have
And all that you are
Believe
And changes
Will
Come

---

[⊕] From "Prayer In Poetry For The Christian Mother".
Used By Permission. Copyright ©2008 V. Andriotis

## THERE I AM[⊕]

Look behind you
There I Am
All around you
There I Am
Close your eyes
There I Am
Why do you seem surprised?

I'm your shadow
There I Am
Right beside you
There I Am
I heard you calling
Here I Am
Your faith has brought Me near

Where shadows find you
Where the moon lights your way
Do not fear the darkness
For there
I'll
Be

---

[⊕] From "Prayer In Poetry For The Christian Mother".
Used By Permission. Copyright ©2008 V. Andriotis

## ALRIGHT[⊕]

That all will be alright
If left in Your hands
Is a reality that must
Be received
Understood
Believed

That all will be alright
If we are ever mindful
That God is at work
Within each
Circumstance
Situation
Encounter
That might present itself
Or that we might find ourselves in

Through prayer
He will enlighten us
Guide us to choices and decisions
That will
Ensure
That all will be
Alright

---

[⊕] From "Prayer In Poetry For The Christian Mother".
Used By Permission. Copyright ©2008 V. Andriotis

## LIMITLESS[⊕]

The world that tells you
The possible
From the impossible
Has not felt hope
Has lost its faith
For with Him
All things are possible
All are limitless

Capable
Incapable
One is simply a boundary of the mind
And of the world
The line between which can be crossed at
any time
By a heart that has been freed
By faith

Nourish your faith
And let
Your world
Be
Limitless

---

[⊕] From "Prayer In Poetry – More Expressions of Faith".
Used By Permission. Copyright ©2009 V. Andriotis

## In This Day, I Pray[⊕]

In this day
I pray, surround me
With the love of a friend
With a word of encouragement
With a warm embrace
And a random kindness

In this day
I pray, that all is right with the world
That our challenges do not exceed our abilities
That the weight of our worries does not exceed
The strength of the shoulders on which they are carried
That a goal
Is always in sight
While another
Is achieved
That our faith in God
Ourselves
And in humanity
Is enough to see us through any day
But our friends remain beside us
Anyway

---

[⊕] From "Prayer In Poetry – More Expressions of Faith". Used By Permission. Copyright ©2009 V. Andriotis

*Prayer in Poetry for the Christian Teenager*

## TO SPEAK TO YOU[⊕]

It is difficult to speak at times
To speak to You
Uncertain
What to say

And so I begin with expressions of gratitude
For all that is
And all that will be

Then
There is my love for You
Ever present
Constant
This I must convey as well

I must tell You of all who are dear to me
And ask that you guide
And protect them

These things I say
These things I pray
And find that they
Are not
So difficult
After all

---

[⊕] From "Prayer In Poetry – More Expressions of Faith". Used By Permission. Copyright ©2009 V. Andriotis

www.ingramcontent.com/pod-product-compliance
Lightning Source LLC
Chambersburg PA
CBHW031415040426
42444CB00005B/580